P9-CEY-500

CURSES!

or ----How Never To Be Foiled Again

CURSES!

or ------How Never To
Be Foiled Again

by STEVE ALLEN

Illustrated by Marvin Rubin

 J. P. Tarcher, Inc., Los Angeles, Calif.
Distributed by Hawthorn Books, Inc., New York

Books by Steve Allen

Bop Fables   Simon and Schuster
Fourteen For Tonight   Henry Holt & Co.
The Funny Men   Simon and Schuster
Wry On The Rocks   Henry Holt & Co.
The Girls On The Tenth Floor   Henry Holt & Co.
The Question Man   Bellmeadow Press, with
                                                  Bernard Geis Assoc.

Mark It And Strike It   Holt, Rinehart & Winston
Not All Of Your Laughter,   Bernard Geis Assoc.
   Not All Of Your Tears
Letter to a Conservative   Doubleday & Co.
The Ground Is Our Table   Doubleday & Co.
Bigger Than A Breadbox   Doubleday & Co.
A Flash Of Swallows   Droke House
The Wake   Doubleday & Co.
Princess Snip-Snip and the   Platt & Munk
   Puppykittens

Copyright © 1973 by Steve Allen. Library of Congress Catalog Card No. 73-76662. ISBN 0-87477-008-4. All rights reserved. Manufactured in the U.S.A.

Published by J. P. Tarcher, Inc. 9110 Sunset Blvd., Los Angeles, CA 90069. Published simultaneously in Canada by Prentice-Hall of Canada, Ltd. 1870 Birchmont Road, Scarborough, Ontario.   1   2   3   4   5   6   7   8   9   10

Designed by Jan Kubota . . . Omega–PAPA

TABLE OF CONTENTS

Introduction	1
Cursing Techniques	7
The Curse: Does It Work?	16
The Anger Of The Ancients	21
The Jewish Verbal Weapon: Humor	27
The Wrath Of Allah	48
Cursing In Church	54
Critical Prayer: Another Name For Cursing?	62
Black Words From The Emerald Isle	66
The Curse Of The Frog	78
Curses From Paradise	81
The Original Curse Of The Gypsy	86

The Curse Of Garra   94

The Skeptics   96

The Curse As A Boomerang   98

A Curse In Rhyme   100

Curses In Which Actions Speak Louder Than Words   103

The Last Word   106

INTRODUCTION

Johnny Carson, playing The Great Carnac, surveys the audience glumly. A joke has just died. Fixing the rubes with a baleful eye, Carnac says, "May the Bird of Paradise fly up your nose."

Don Rickles, perspiring and triumphant, towers over his audience in a swank Las Vegas lounge showroom. A heckler has just had the nerve to cross swords with comedy's ablest put-down artist. "Sir," Rickles shouts, "as you leave this room tonight—may a rash cover your entire body."

Hundreds of miles to the west heavy curtains are drawn to keep the mid-afternoon sun out of a San Fernando Valley home. A fierce-faced young woman sits before a coffee table staring into the flame of a scented candle as she sticks a hatpin repeatedly into the small effigy of a man she hates.

"May a hot, searing pain strike your entrails," *she hisses.*

Carson and Rickles are kidding; the young woman is deadly serious. But all three are using a weapon that the civilized world has long assumed was only a relic of a primitive and superstitious past: the curse. Whether it reflects humor or hate, like other aspects of man's mysterious past cursing is still with us.

But alas, the art of cursing has fallen on evil days. "Drop dead" and the ever-popular "_____ you" can't begin to compete with the rich images of ancient curses and the vigor of ethnic ones.

Some are old—
  "May the day you were born be erased from the calendar." (Book of Job)

3

Some are new—
"May your sex life be as good as your credit." (J. Corigan)

Some are borrowed—
"May you suffer the one thing in the world worse than being talked about—and that is not being talked about." (Oscar Wilde)

Some blue—
"May you be up to your ass in alligators." (Cajun)

4

Some curse the body—
"You should fall down the stairs and break every tooth in your jaw except one, and in that one you should have a toothache for the rest of your life."

Some curse the mind—
"May you be cursed with a chronic anxiety about the weather." (John Burroughs)

Others curse the spirit—
"A down mouth be yours." (Scottish Highlands)

And even the pocketbook—
"Your creditors should always have your current address."

Curses can be painful—
"May you fall into the hands of a farsighted dentist."

Picturesque—
"May you be so bald, flies use your head for ice shows."

Or just plain doleful—
"Everything you take in your hands should be hot, and everything you take in your arms should be cold."

There are curses that not only condemn, but insult as well:

"You should be hanging from the edge of a cliff while your mother tries to remember your father's name."

"May your finger get stuck in your nose." **(Polish)**

I would like to think of this guide to verbal vengeance as a public service which will bring cursing back to the artistic and literary level it once enjoyed. By following the how-to-do-it instructions on page 109, you can participate in this rebirth.

Bless you!

Cursing Techniques

(A Glossary of Terms)

Cursing is the expression of a wish that misfortune, evil, doom, calamity, or utter destruction befall another person. It also describes the act of reciting a formula or charm intended to cause such misfortune to another.

7

Swearing

is committing
one's self to a vow or
promise with an appeal to some
superhuman being. When swearing involves
the heartfelt wish to inflict evil on another, it becomes a curse.

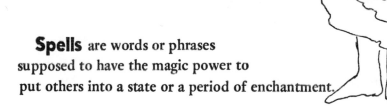

Spells are words or phrases
supposed to have the magic power to
put others into a state or a period of enchantment.

9

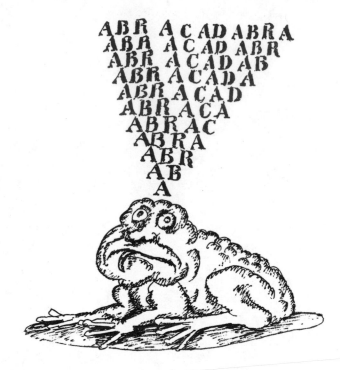

Incantations are chantings of words said to have magical power.

10

The Evil Eye is rooted in the superstitious belief that some people can cause harm just by looking. This strange belief has existed for thousands of years in many parts of the world, and still has followers in southern Europe and the Middle East. Believers may try to counteract the effects of the evil eye by reciting magic words, pointing with a prong of coral, or wearing charms.

Charms are trinkets or amulets worn on chains, bracelets, etc., for supposed magical effect. In addition, any action that is thought to have magical power (the chanting or recitation of a magic verse or formula) is called a charm.

Hex is a term that originated in the United States, and means casting an evil eye, or putting a curse on.

Voodoo is one of the religious beliefs of certain African natives. The word means Spirit or God. As practiced in the West Indies and a few areas of the United States, voodoo includes the pursuit of magic and contains some elements borrowed from the Catholic religion. Its devotees believe that spirits of the dead live in a world of ghosts, but can visit the world of the living to bless or curse people. If a man makes a wax image of his enemy and sticks pins into it, he is practicing voodoo to injure his enemy.

14

Witchcraft is the practice of evil acts by witches (generally women) or people supposed to have evil power. This power is believed to have been given, or sold, by devils, and a witch calls upon spirits or demons to rise up and hurt her enemies. Sometimes a witch is said to lay a curse by using parings of the victim's fingernails, a lock of his hair, or a piece of clothing. In times long gone people used to destroy their nail parings and hair clippings in order to keep from being cursed.

The Curse: Does It Work?

Wise old sayings are frequently noteworthy for their lack of wisdom. For example, "Sticks and stones may break my bones, but names will never hurt me." Verbal attack obviously can do great damage, as the laws of slander and libel suggest. Few of us can go for 24 hours without being hurt to at least some degree by the words of others. Aggressive comments by friends or enemies can even have physically destructive effects.

Superstitious and primitive as voodoo is, there is undeniable evidence that those who believe in it do indeed fall ill as a result of the curses and spells of their enemies. Some students of voodoo cults attribute the sufferings of the victims purely to the power of suggestion, the same force summoned up by vaudeville hypnotists in producing their remarkable effects. In other words, if a man learns that his enemy has cast a hateful spell on him, he may suffer because he believes that it is reasonable for him to do so.

But some observers of the occult say that voodoo spells can be harmful even when the victim knows nothing of them; that there are dark forces which can be summoned up even without the conscious knowledge of the person who suffers and, in some cases, dies. I would have to see a considerable body of evidence before I could accept this, but it would be a mistake to assume it is a belief shared only by backward natives in jungles and mountain villages of underdeveloped nations.

THE CEREMONY OF THE VOODOO CURSE

Not long ago a man named Anton Szandor La Vey appeared on my television program. If you saw the motion picture, *Rosemary's Baby,* you will already have met Mr. La Vey: he played the role of Satan in the film. In real life he claims to have the same relation with the devil that Christians have with Christ. He is, in fact, considered the "Black Pope" of the Church of Satan in San Francisco. It is difficult to say whether he is carrying off one of the century's more successful put ons or is entirely sincere in his peculiar beliefs. Most of the members of our

TV production staff, as well as our studio audience, regarded him skeptically and laughed at some of his more remarkable observations.

But apparently the members of his Church, as well as readers of his various books, take him seriously. In *The Compleat Witch . . . or What To Do When Virtue Fails,* La Vey talks about the various ways to curse your enemies "using the powers of ceremonial magic." He says that pictures, photos, wax or clay models of the intended victim can be used, but the device he recommends is "a handmade doll, similar in construction to those used in the use of voodoo magic." Why? Well, because "the voodoo doll has become synonymous with cursing, and if for no other reason than this ready-made association, such an effigy should be used."

He goes on to emphasize the importance of making your own voodoo doll, "as the creative energy you expend fashioning the doll will definitely add to the effectiveness of your ritual." The best color, he adds, "is the basic color of the victim's skin." Apparently you can make a very effective doll from a pair of socks, but there is one important proviso: "Whatever you do, don't use material that you have worn from which to fashion the doll, nor salvage material from clothing worn by anyone for whom you care. . . ."

The next step is to supply the head of the doll with the face of one's enemy—"or at least a reasonable facsimile." Then you put the finished doll aside for 24 hours, "if possible in a place where you cannot fail to see it, and this will allow the anticipation of what you are about to do to become intensified by the anger engendered by being confronted with your enemy."

At the end of 24 hours you prepare to stick pins or nails into the doll. According to La Vey, "the use of nails rather than pins is recommended." Also, "it is wise to ascertain the victim's weak spots healthwise" and, finally, "it is best to perform this ritual in complete privacy, as it is serious business." Mr. La Vey concludes: "If done properly, it is not necessary that your victim have any knowledge of your curse."

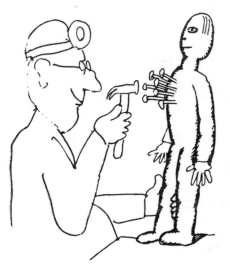

The Anger Of The Ancients

Once primitive man had even the vaguest idea about the supernatural, it didn't take him long to figure out that when he could not hit back at his enemies by hurling sticks and stones, he might at least use words calculated to invite the gods to do his enemies harm.

The Egyptians in particular were cursers extraordinary, as we see from the inscription written on a mortuary statue of Ursu, an engineer who lived shortly before the time of the boy pharaoh, Tutankhamen:

"He who trespasses upon my property, or who shall injure my tomb, or drag out my mummy, the Sun-god shall punish him. He shall not bequeath his goods to his children; his heart shall not have pleasure in life; he shall not receive water (for his spirit to drink) in the tomb; and his soul shall be destroyed forever."

Now there's a man who didn't like being disturbed!

If you think that that kind of cursing doesn't work, consider the fate of Lord Carnarvon who ignored the following inscription on Tutankhamen's tomb:

"Death shall come on swift wings to him who disturbs the sleep of pharaoh."

Carnarvon, who financed the expedition that found and opened the tomb, died from an infected mosquito bite shortly after the pharaoh's treasure was discovered.

In India, the Toda tribe used this ceremonial curse to anticipate the mischief that someone might do to the sacred cattle:

"Die, may he: Tiger, catch him: Snake, bite him: Steep hill, fall down on him: River, flow over him: Wild boar, bite him."

A form of this imprecation existed in many ancient languages:

"May you never see a son to follow your body to the grave, or a daughter to mourn your death."

But it was Confucius who, in his sophistication, managed to invoke the most chilling torment:

"May you be born in an important time."

the jewish verbal weapon: humor

The ancient Hebrews believed in one God, and this complicated their cursing. The Third Commandment, which explicitly forbade Jews to take the Lord's name in vain, made the serious invocation of heavenly anger a seldom-used tool.

Indeed, in the Talmud there is proof of the importance which the Jews of thousands of years ago attached to the prohibition on the use of the Lord's name for purposes other than spiritual worship or respect. These ancient prohibitions stemmed not from the mere belief that it was disrespectful, but that it was a thoughtless use of an *authentic power.*

That the curse was common in ancient times, however, is clear from the many Biblical references to the practice. Some of them, by the way, give rise to an interesting theological puzzle in that God himself is quoted as having cursed people and things.

The Lord said in his heart, "I will never again curse the ground because of man, for the imagination of man's heart is evil from his youth." (Genesis 8:21.)

Now the Lord said to Abram, "And I will make of you a great nation, and I will bless you, and make your name great so that you will be a blessing. And I will bless those that bless you, and him who curses you I will curse." (Genesis 12:3.)

To the Jew in the European ghetto thousands of years later, life was unbearably frustrating, and cursing became an important safety valve.

Some of the Jews' traditional Yiddish expletives were simple invocations of calamity upon their tormentors:

> *"You should know from bad."*

> *"Sickness should catch up with you."*

> *"A heavy weight should descend on your heart."*

> *"A darkness should descend on you."*

But many of the classic curses were so thoroughly violent that they became funny, and diffused the anger of the oppressed curser:

"You should choke on a pudding."

"You should be like a chandelier, hung by day and burned by night."

"You should have a child through the ribs."

"You should lie in the deepest hell."

"You should be torn apart."

"You should burn like a candle."

"Your intestines should crawl out."

"Your tongue should dry out."

"You should fall off a church spire."

"You should become pregnant with toothpicks."

"Pieces should f a l l off from you."

"A devil should ride on top of your father's father."

"It should ring from your ears continuously."

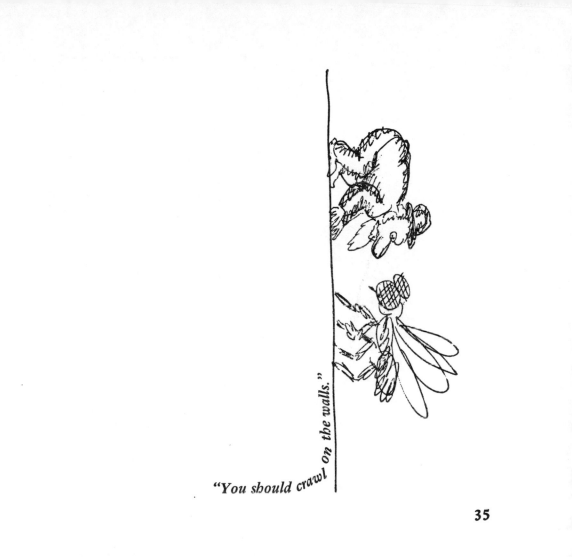

"You should crawl on the walls."

"Your intestines should boil like a samovar."

"You should swell up like a mountain."

37

Some of the Yiddish curses relieved the tension by projecting a foolish picture of the enemy:

"You should grow like a turnip—with the head down and the roots up."

"May you choke on your eyelash."

"May your teeth grow longer than your beard."

"May a tree grow up in your hand."

"Corns should grow on your nose."

"You should become a head shorter."

"Your nose should drip like my faucet."

"Your beard should grow upward and cover your face."

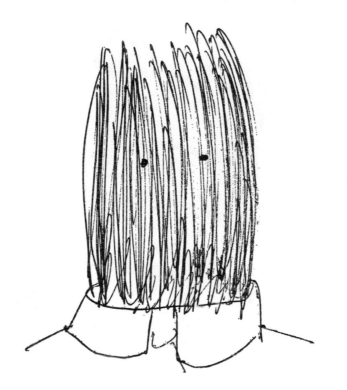

"It should stink from your nose."

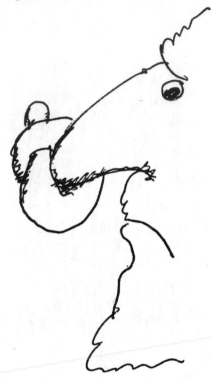

"Your head should shrink to the size of a peanut."

41

"It should smell from your head like it smells from my feet."

"*A hernia should grow on your head.*"

"Beets should grow in your stomach and you should urinate borscht."

Although the Yiddish curses were full of bitterness, their joke-like character indicates that the Jews didn't have too much faith in the results. The curses of these European Jews seem to have been intended to get the venom out of their systems. In other words, they were aids to Jewish mental health.

It was at those moments when no humor could be found in the situation that the Yiddish curses became heartbreaking. The most devastating thing a ghetto Jew could wish on his foe was: "My troubles on your head."

For some reason, there are a few Jewish curses that sound better in the original Yiddish.

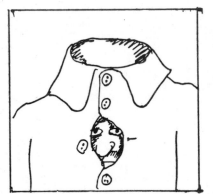

Du zolst vern mit a kup kurtzer.

(You should be a head shorter.)

Meine tzores oif dein kup!

(My troubles on your head.)

For instance, "Ver farblunzhet" is much more effective than "You should get lost," and "Gai grub chrain" is much more meaningful than "You should go dig horseradish," and certainly "In dread mit di baener" would work, while one might doubt the efficacy of "May your bones be in the ground."

Zul dir rinen fun dein nuz vi es rint fun mein krant.

(Your nose should drip like my faucet.)

Zolst hangen mit'n kup arup!

(You should hang with your head upside down!)

The Wrath Of Allah

The Prophet Mohammed called cursing the 8th infirmity of the tongue, and indicated that cursing an animal, a man or even an object was severely reprehensible.

"Invoke not upon each other of you Allah's curse or His wrath."

Clearly, calling down Allah's curse on another was a perilous undertaking, and the Prophet himself received a heavenly reprimand when he indulged in it.

He detailed sound reasons why condemning anyone in the name of Allah was not only blasphemous arrogance, but nonsense. In the first place, no believing Muslim may be safely cursed, for the mere profession of the Islamic faith confers upon him Allah's mercy. It is not even considered safe to curse an unbeliever, for one day he may embrace Islam. It is additionally dangerous to say, "Allah curse him so long as he remains in his unbelief," for the implication then is "Allah cause him to *remain* an unbeliever, so that this curse may maintain its hold upon him," and, of course, it's a deadly sin for a Muslim to advocate unbelief, even for an unbeliever.

Islam is a practical religion, and doesn't generally place unbearable demands upon man's mind or body. Therefore if one *must* condemn another party in Allah's name there is a formula to be followed.

A true believer is free to curse certain *groups of people* (wholesale, as it were—Jews, Christians, Zoroastrians, unbelievers, oppressors, etc. It is quite certain that while an individual Jew or Christian, for example, may someday be converted to Islam, *all* Jews or Christians never will).

The cursing of an individual signifies driving him away from Allah and, therefore, is not permitted *except* when directed to a person who has undeniably estranged himself from Allah forever. Since live people may change their status at any time, the only safe individual curses are those where the particular person's guilt is a historical fact attested to by tradition. It's even safer when the individual has been known to die in Allah's disfavor. ("Pharaoh—Allah curse him!")

51

And so it is that a tradition of Arab curses developed that did not involve Allah. They range from an angry wish that one's enemy would come to suffer physical affliction:

"May your left ear wither and fall into your right pocket."

—to the heartfelt hope that the victim might have to endure a fate worse than no life after death:

"May the sweat of a thousand camels infest your armpits."

Cursing In Church

Although at first it might seem that cursing has no proper connection with religion, the fact is that cursing and religion have been closely connected throughout history. For while religion has usually sought to promote what it considered to be virtue, the very reason for its emphasis on virtue was the existence of evil. There would be no need for a commandment such as "Thou shalt not kill" were it not that men have slaughtered each other for millions of years.

Cursing, then, is essentially a substitute for direct physical aggression. And it is a substitute which involves serious moral questions, as is suggested by the commandment which forbids the taking of the Lord's name in vain.

The New Testament includes several direct references to cursing. Oddly enough, Christ himself invoked a curse:

"Now in the morning as Jesus returned into the city, he hungered. And when he saw a fig tree in the way, he came to it, and found nothing thereon but leaves only, and said unto it, 'Let no fruit grow on thee henceforward forever.' And presently the fig tree withered away." (Matthew 21:18-21)

In general, however, the New Testament condemns cursing and advocates turning the other cheek. As Jesus said, "Love your enemies and pray for those who curse you." (Matthew 5: 44)

Centuries later the Catholic and Eastern Churches employed ritual cursing as a means of excommunicating the unfaithful. Sir Thomas Malory was referring to excommunication when he wrote in the *Morte d'Arthur,* "I shall curse you with Bell, and Book and Candle."

These three symbols occur often in literature, but never as amusingly as in *The Jackdaw of Rheims* by R. H. Barham, which is a take off on the famous "Curse of Bishop Ernulf" preserved in the Cathedral at Rochester, England:

"The Cardinal rose with a dignified look.
He call'd for his candle, his bell and his book!
　　In holy anger, and pious grief,
　　He solemnly cursed that rascally thief!
He cursed him at board, he cursed him in bed;
From the sole of his foot to the crown of his head;
He cursed him in sleeping, that every night
He should dream of the devil, and wake in a fright!
He cursed him in eating, he cursed him in drinking,
He cursed him in coughing, in sneezing, in winking;
He cursed him in sitting, in standing, in lying;
He cursed him in living, he cursed him in dying.
　　Never was heard such a terrible curse!
　　　　But what gave rise
　　　　To no little surprise,
　　Nobody seem'd one penny the worse!"

A real curse of excommunication rendered from the Chair of Pope Clement VI in the 14th century was:

"Let him be damned in his going out and coming in. The Lord strike him with madness and blindness and mental insanity. May the heavens empty upon him thunderbolts and the wrath of the Omnipotent burn itself unto him in the present and future world. May the Universe light against him and the earth open to swallow him up!"

The Church of England is said to have posted signs that read:

"Cursed are the unmerciful, the fornicators, adulterers, covetous persons, idolaters, philanderers, slanderers, drunkards, and extortioners."

You can't say that the Church didn't give fair warning. Obviously the record of human behavior over the past several thousand years shows that as a deterrent the curse was an utter failure.

S. N. Shirley of Littlerock, California has provided me with a pamphlet that reproduces an ancient curse of excommunication apparently employed by the Catholic Church and perhaps other Christian churches as well. While the curse is too lengthy to reproduce in full, the following excerpts give an indication of its vigor and heat:

"We excommunicate and anathematize him from the threshold of the Holy Church of God Almighty.

"We sequester him, that he may be tormented . . .

"May the Father, who creates man, curse him!

"May the Son, who suffered for us, curse him!

"May the Holy Ghost, who is poured out in baptism, curse him!

"May the Holy Cross, which Christ for our salvation, triumphing over His enemies, ascended, curse him!

"May the Holy Mary, ever Virgin and the Mother of God. curse him!

"May all the Angels, Principalities and Powers, and all Heavenly Armies curse him!

"May the glorious band of the Patriarchs and Prophets curse him! . . .

"May all the Saints, from the beginning of the world to everlasting ages who are found to be beloved of God, damn him!"

Critical Prayer: Another Name For Cursing?

One of the difficulties involved with research into occult matters is knowing where to place sharply defined boundaries. Is there a fundamental distinction between a prayer and a curse, or are they both appeals to precisely the same forces, invoked for opposite ends?

One of the most interesting reports of apparently reliable research, supported by extensive laboratory experiments, is *The Power of Prayer on Plants* by Rev. Franklin Loehr.

Most thoughtful readers will without doubt approach his account with a strong skeptical bias, but Dr. Loehr is not an itinerant tea-leaf reader or fortune teller. He is a distinguished Presbyterian minister, trained in chemistry. His studies of psychosomatic medicine convinced him that the mind had more remarkable powers than are commonly recognized.

When in 1952 Dr. J. B. Rhine of the parapsychology laboratory at Duke University conducted experiments with plants to test the efficacy of prayer, Dr. Loehr and his colleagues at the Religious Research Foundation decided to undertake similar research.

The methodology involved was simple. A number of seeds were planted, and all were given precisely equal treatment, with one exception. Half the seeds were given prayer, the other half were not. At certain points growth of the seeds was carefully measured and results compared. Although it seems incredible that thinking favorably about a plant, or speaking words of encouragement to it, or asking a Divinity to intervene on its behalf, could affect its growth, the studies by Loehr's group apparently demonstrated that prayed-for plants enjoyed significantly more vigorous growth than un-prayed-for plants.

An aspect of the group's research relates directly to the subject of cursing. As Loehr explains it:

"The next major lesson we learned is that prayer not only can stimulate growth but, when properly applied, *can repress and even turn back plant growth.* (Italics added.)

"Erwin Prust of Pasadena, a businessman and early member of the Religious Research Foundation, first showed us this power of prayer. He cut six slips of ivy of equal length and leafage from his own backyard fence. With a small trowel he dug a bit of dirt, mixed it, and filled two pots. He put three ivy slips in each pot, then took them to his wife. She chose one to get prayer for growth, which Mr. Prust then marked with a *plus* sign. He marked the other with a *minus* sign to indicate *prayer for non-growth*." (Italics added.)

Then Prust started prayer work on both. They received the same treatment—water, sunshine, placement, warmth, etc.—except for a difference in the prayer given them.

At first all the ivy took root and started to grow. At the end of the first week there was little evident difference. But after two weeks a difference was noted. The growth-prayer plants were thriving, but the non-growth prayer plants were beginning to droop. Prust continued his experiment for five weeks, at the end of which the non-growth prayer plants were dead.

"The special experiments with prayer for non-growth," Dr. Loehr observes, "may have significance for such human afflictions as cancer. Cancer is an unwanted growth of the human body. If we can stop the growth of plants, and even turn it back, by prayer in a laboratory, we may be on the way to discovering more about prayer as a force in human beings."

Black Words From The Emerald Isle

There is a strange opinion to be found in Ireland upon the subject of curses. A curse, the peasants say, will rest for seven years in the air, ready to land on the head of the victim. It hovers over him like a kite, waiting for the moment when he may be abandoned by his guardian angel; then it shoots with the rapidity of a meteor onto his head, and clings to him in the shape of illness, temptation, or some other calamity.

Many Irish curses are difficult to understand because they have their origin in some historical event—sometimes obscure—or in poetical metaphors that require a particular bit of knowledge. For example:

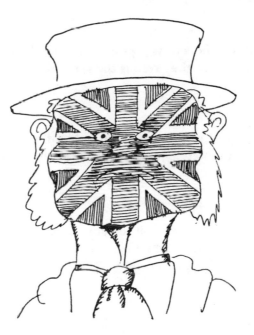

"The Curse of Cromwell on you!"—still used today—means that you should suffer as the Irish did under the rule of Cromwell.

"The curse o' the crows upon you!" is thought to relate to the Danish invasion, since the raven is the symbol of Denmark.

"Six eggs to you, and half-a-dozen o' them rotten!" is a kind of curse used in good-humored banter, as retaliation when presented with a disappointment.

"May you never die till you see your own funeral" suggests that you should be hanged, for then you will be favored with a view of the crowd and much of the spectacle.

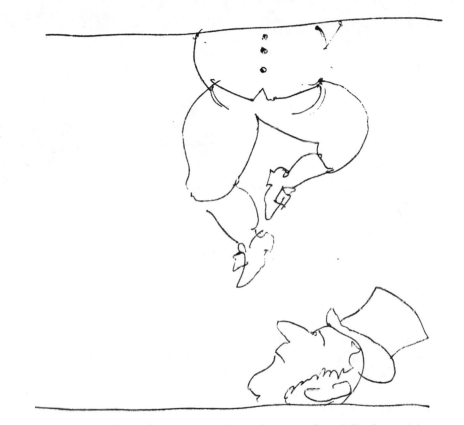

"May your last dance be a hornpipe on the air" also wishes you
hanged.

The Irish are somewhat unique in believing that the blessing of one person may cancel the curse of another. Indeed, the Irish may well have had a hand in creating the old folk legend of "Sleeping Beauty," for as the story goes, a bad fairy, not invited to the christening of the king's baby daughter, came to the party anyway and said that the new princess would prick her finger and die. Subsequently a good fairy, who had not yet blessed the child, countered the curse by saying that the princess would not die, but would merely sleep for 100 years.

But the real and heartfelt curses of the Irish, although poetically phrased, are as direct as the maledictions of all peoples throughout the world:

"May you melt off the earth like snow off the ditch!"

While writing this book, I happened to mention on my television show that I was looking for examples of curses. As a result, I received an interesting letter from Mrs. Corrina K. Richey of San Pedro, California:

"... Several years ago I worked with a man who used—profusely—the curse that I am submitting to you. You could gauge the temperature of his anger by the volume and the verbal punctuation:

> *'May the curse of Mary Malone and her nine blind,*
> *illegitimate children chase you so far over the hills*
> *of Damnation that Jesus Christ Himself can't find*
> *you with a telescope!'* "

Will Millar, of The Irish Rovers, told me of a cursing song called:

NELL FLAHERTY'S DRAKE

"Bad wind to the robber—be he drunk or sober
that murdered Nell Flaherty's beautiful drake.
May his pig never grunt.
May his cat never hunt.
May a ghost ever hunt him at dead of night.
May his hen never lay, may his ass never bray.
May his goat fly away like an old paper kite.
That the flies and the fleas may the wretch ever tease.
May the piercing March breeze make him shiver and shake.
May a lump of a stick raise bumps fast and thick
on the monster that murdered Nell Flaherty's Drake.

May his spade never dig.
May his sow never pig.
May each hair in his wig be well thrashed with a flail.
May his door never latch.
May his house have no thatch.
May his turkeys not hatch.
May the rats eat his mail.
May every old fairy from Cork to Dunleary
dip him snug and airy in river or lake
where the eel and the trout may dine on the snout
of the monster that murdered Nell Flaherty's Drake."

The most famous Irish curse is "May she marry a ghost, and bear him a kitten and may the high king of glory permit it to get the mange." Those were originally the last lines of a poem called "Righteous Anger," which tells a bitter story through the eyes of a man who has just been thrown out of his favorite pub, recently taken over by a new owner.

RIGHTEOUS ANGER

The lanky hank of a she in the Inn over there
Nearly kilt me for askin' the lend of a glass of beer.
May the devil grasp the whey-faced slut by the hair
And beat bad manners out of her skin for a year.

The parboiled imp with the hardest jar I've ever seen
        in virtue's path
Came runtin' and ragin' the minute she looked at me
And threw me out of the house on the back of me head.

Now, if I had asked her master, he would have given me a cask a day
But her with the beer at hand, not one gill would arrange.
May she marry a ghost, and bear him a kitten
And may the high king of glory permit it to get the mange.

The Curse Of The Frog

All of the following French curses come from the same source: a superb comic actor named Pierre Olaf. I've never been able to locate any other French curses, in spite of repeated efforts to do so.

These impish (if somewhat painful) images may reflect the basic nature of the French peasant—or they may only reflect the imp that most certainly can be found in Pierre. Some, said to be French country curses, wouldn't be too pleasant in the city either:

"May you pee vinegar all night."

"May the devil prick your bottom with forks."

79

This one refers to the wild boars that once roamed the roads, plaguing travelers:

*"May little pigs eat
you on your journey."*

As a lad, Pierre made up this curse:

"May the math teacher come down with the mumps."

But he has assured me that he knows from personal experience this curse doesn't work!

Curses From Paradise

The traditional curses from the South Pacific don't travel well. Since our cultural background does not include cannibalism, we aren't terribly impressed by threats, oaths and curses such as:

"Go cook your father." (Maori)

Interestingly enough, there was only one insult considered worse than that. It is:

"Go cook your grandfather."

The other Polynesian and Melanesian island cultures also reflect this preoccupation:

"You will bake your grandfather 'til his skin turns to cracknel, and gnaw his skull for your share." (Tonga)

"Your skull be my calabash."

"My fork is your bone."

"You are a dead man's bone."

"Dig up your father by moonlight and make soup of his bones." (Fiji Islands)

The Samoan Island curses tend to deal with eating and being eaten, even when the imagery is not cannibalistic in the strict sense:

"May fire blast the eyes of the thief who stole my bananas."

"Evil shall devour you."

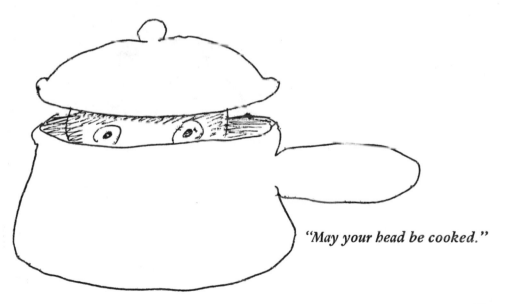

"May your head be cooked."

"May the thief be eaten by a white shark."

But in the strict social structure in which the New Zealand Maoris lived, cursing another person is considered more of a sin than cannibalism:

"Let the head of the curser be baked in the oven, served up as food for me, dead and gone to the night."

The Original Curse Of The Gypsy

Gypsies wander the face of the earth—it is said—because of a curse placed on their Chief by their number one sorcerer. The Chief had committed the ultimate "no-no" of marrying his sister. Here then is the original Curse of the Gypsy:

"May you wander over the face of the earth forever, never sleep twice in the same place, never drink water twice from the same well, and never cross the same river twice in a year."

The following are almost accurate gypsy curses, changed slightly by an American gypsy, so that their awful power won't affect you as you read them. These curses are said to be so potent they should never be read aloud unless you really mean business.

When a gypsy wants to put a curse on someone who might wish to steal the gypsy's goods (for example, if she has to leave her crystal ball, scarf or wagon in an unprotected place) she says:

"Thy hands and thy feet shall soon decay,
If thou takest my goods away!"

Here is a curse for a woman to put on a rival who has robbed her of her man. It is the worst curse a woman can invoke, because it denies another the power to return love. I would tell you what root to plant in order to make this curse work, but I think I'd better not.

"As this root grows, like flesh and bone,
May your heart be ever turned to stone."

Here's the gypsy way to curse a lover who is marrying someone else:
You try to get a hair from his head, and thread a needle with it.
Then you take a candle and light it. You prick the
candle three times, with the needle going down
away from the flame, and you say,
"Thrice the candle broke by me,
thrice thy heart shall
broken be."

The gypsy woman's pride is her hair. She puts coins in it to show her wealth, grease to keep her warm, and her greatest fear is of losing it. To curse a woman thoroughly, so that her hair will be so knotted that she will have to shave it off, one would say:

"Wind on the sea, tidal wave of foam,
Tangles in her hair, she can never comb."

To deliver the ultimate curse, gypsies say:

> *"Chairs, tables, knives, forks,*
> *Tankards, bottles, cups, corks,*
> *Dishes, beds, boots and keg,*
> *Bacon, pudding, milk and egg,*
> *Every pillow, sheet and bed,*
> *The dough in the trough, and the baked bread,*
> *Every bit of provender on the shelf,*
> *And all you will have left is the house itself!"*

But their strongest threat is:

> *"May you be cursed by a gypsy who stutters!"*

The Curse Of Garra

Ripley's *Believe It Or Not Ghost Stories and Plays* tells of the oasis of Garra in the Libyan Desert, in North Africa, which was cursed more than three centuries ago. The malediction, it is said, still blights the life of its inhabitants. The men of Garra committed an unpardonable act of sacrilege by waylaying and robbing a caravan of Mecca-bound pilgrims. The leader of the caravan, a venerable old man named Abdel Sayed, pronounced the curse: that there should never be more than forty men alive in Garra at the same time.

According to Ripley,

"In World War I, an Australian military detachment, numbering 18 men, was temporarily stationed in Garra. The Aussies had hardly arrived when an epidemic struck the native population and 18 deaths occurred—to restore the balance."

The Skeptics

Just as records of religious literature are full of atheistic and agnostic speculation, so the literature of curses includes many examples of skepticism:

"A thousand curses never tore a shirt." (Syrian)

"Curses hurt not: prayers injure not." (German)

"Cussin' de weather is mighty po' farmin'." (Early American Negro)

Lord Carnarvon (see p. 22) apparently was not consulted concerning these views.

The Curse As A Boomerang

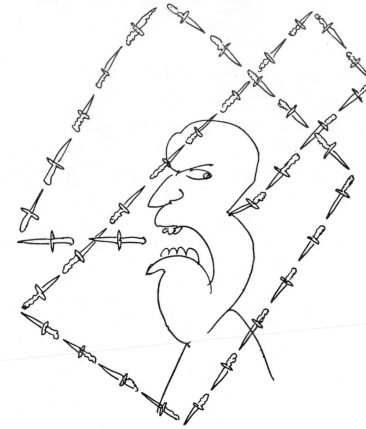

The concept that there is an inherent danger in wishing ill on another is found in all cultures—Biblical, Melanesian, European—and is not limited to those instances where the Deity's name is invoked.

It is generally considered that the curser sours his personality and his relationship with the world around him:

"Lips that curse shall want bread." (Polish)

"I have heard it said that a curse was like a stone flung up to the heavens, and mayest return on the head that sent it." (Scott)

"A curse sticks to no one but the curser." (German)

"May your curses, like chickens, come home to roost: they shall return to you as birds to their nest." (Cajun warning)

So watch it!

The Curse In Rhyme

*"Curst be the verse, how well soe'er it flow,
That tends to make one worthy man my foe."*
(Alexander Pope)

The rhymed form of a curse or spell was considered particularly magical. The hypnotic effect of the music of the incantation, and the non-workaday nature of the form itself, united to give additional mystique to the rhymed curse. In addition, curses in verse were passed on through the generations because a rhyme scheme made a curse much easier to remember, and much harder for the victim to forget.

> *"I am a rimer of the Irish race,*
> *and have already rimed thee staring mad:*
> *but if thou ceast not thy bold jests to spread,*
> *I'll never leave thee till I have rimed thee dead."*
>
> *(Satirical Elizabethan curse)*

The gypsies did much of their cursing in rhyme. To curse an unfaithful lover, they would chant:

> *"A lying heart and devil's eyes*
> *Always false and full of lies,*
> *Cursed to be ever poor, and never wise."*

The rhymed epitaph on Shakespeare's tombstone in Stratford Church is said to have been chosen by him, but is not from his pen—and the last line is an imitation of the damnation clause so frequent in Roman sepulchral inscriptions:

"Good frend for Jesvs sake forbeare,
To digg the dust encloased heare.
Blest be ye man yt spares the stones
And curst be he yt moves my bones."

Curses In Which Actions Speak Louder Than Words

Throughout the primitive world techniques were developed for condemning those considered wrongdoers. These involved magical motions similar to those used by practitioners of voodoo. Instead of requiring nail parings, hair clippings or miniature forms of the victim, however, these less complex actions utilized everyday objects at hand.

In Borneo, if one wanted to condemn a liar, and involve others in order to add weight to the condemnation, the following threat was issued:

> *"Let anyone who does not add to this liar's heap suffer from pains in the head."*

At this, everyone would throw sticks in a pile and the pile would be called by the liar's name, which would lead to his shame.

A very old Irish technique for causing enmity between sweethearts instructed one to take a handful of clay from a newly-made grave and shake it between the lovers, saying:

> *"Hate ye, one another! May ye be as hateful to each other as sin is to Christ, as bread, eaten without a blessing, is to God."*

In Tuscany, an ancient curse involved the throwing of a stone:

"I cast not away this stone, but cast away the well-being and good fortune of (name) *so that his well-being should flow away like the coursing water, so that he may no longer enjoy any good."*

The Last Word

It can be safely assumed that a certain amount of cursing is going to take place despite all religious prohibitions and it can be fairly argued that whatever is considered worth doing is worth doing well.

If the reader is personally determined to contribute to a revival of the lost art of cursing then it is essential that imagination be brought into play.

Consider the two curses most commonly heard at present: "Go to hell!" (short for "You should go to hell") and "Go ———— yourself!" (a contraction of "You should go ———— yourself").

Each imprecation not only reveals a singular lack of creativity but, perhaps more importantly, neither works.

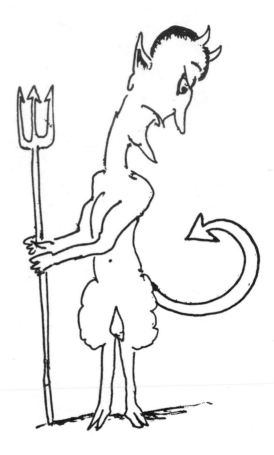

As regards the first, few people seem any longer to believe in hellfire and as for the second it is a physical impossibility; though no doubt some enterprising pornographer will shortly produce a film about the attempt.

Such considerations aside, almost everyone would agree that cursing, however deplorable, is a means of attack much less dangerous to both curser and cursee than its immediate alternative, physical attack.

I mean, which would you prefer, (A) to have a man say, "May your head fall off," or (B) to have him *knock* it off?

Let us assume then that despite all commandments of God and man to the contrary, you are determined to curse somebody. Then the least you can do is be methodical about it.

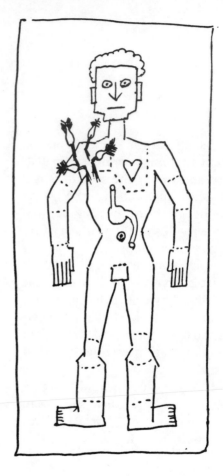

BODY PARTS TO CURSE

Is there any body area of the hated one that seems to you the most likely specific target? In case you have not had recent occasion to take inventory of the most curseable human parts, here is a convenient list, which you might want to carry in your handbag or wallet for use when seized by fits of fury on the freeway, at the bank, while watching television, hearing a presidential press conference, or whatever:

Windpipe	Belly-button
Eyelids	Nostrils
Inside of the mouth	Tooth root canals
Between the toes	Backside
Liver	Sex organs
Fingernails	Hair follicles
Lips	Bone marrow
Brain	Achilles tendon
Armpit	Small of the back

If you are gripped not only by anger but also by envy, which is often the case with cursing-types, then you might want to invoke your curse on that portion of your enemy's person that he might be most proud of. If he has a large, bushy Afro, for example—which many whites as well as blacks presently sport—you might say,

"When you wake up in the morning may you look less like Angela Davis and more like Yul Brynner!"

Or, if you are a modestly endowed young lady jealous of a buxom rival, you might say,

"When you take off your clothes tonight may your chest look like that of Don Knotts!"

OTHER CURSEABLE ASPECTS OF LIFE

For the squeamish, invoking the wrath of God-knows-what on somebody else's *body* may seem a bit much. There are, fortunately, hundreds of other things on which a curse may properly be placed.

Consider, for instance, the cursee's:

front lawn
golf clubs
underwear
contact lenses
shoelaces
automobile
food in the refrigerator
roof during a rainstorm
fountain pen in the pocket
    of his best suit
septic tank

WHAT YOU WANT TO HAPPEN

Once you have decided what aspect of the cursee's life you are going to attack, you must decide what you wish to happen to it. Below is a list of dreadful things the unimaginative might consider:

"Your _____ should _____."

get stuffed up
be run over by a steam roller
have a spasm
go flat
get caught in a revolving door

blow away
get the crud
turn green and fall off
have a wart
be forgotten
turn against you

If there is nothing appropriate on the above list, consult your own inherent viciousness for something even more diabolical.

COMPOUND IT

Things can be made even worse if they can be made to take place in an uncomfortable or embarrassing location.

LIST OF BAD LOCATIONS

Macy's window
the Chicago stockyards
a glue factory
on the edge of a
    volcano
a tankful of piranhas

the coach lounge of a 747
a traffic jam
under a leaky crankcase
on a Greyhound bus with a carsick
    Scout troop
an Italian airport

Things can also be made worse in regard to the *time-scale*. For instance,

LIST OF BAD TIMES

forever
forever-and-a-day
in the next ten seconds
on your 40th birthday
never
New Year's Day
at three in the morning
on the first night of your honeymoon
till hell freezes over

Note: TAKE THE CURSEE BY SURPRISE

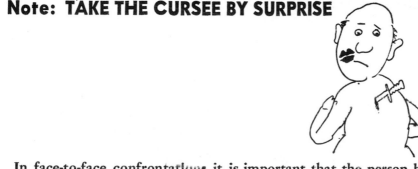

In face-to-face confrontations it is important that the person being cursed remain unaware that you are about to lay one on him. If you can start your curse, therefore, with a seeming compliment, his ego will be undefended from your attack.

For instance, to an insomniac you might say:

"When you fall asleep . . . may you dream that you are awake."

To a compulsive eater, you could remark:

"You should be eating a big bun with raisins . . . and the raisins should fly away."

To a person of unusually sour disposition, you can say:

"May you soon have reason to smile . . . and as soon as you do, may you swallow your ear."

CURSES FOR SPECIAL OCCASIONS

Almost every special occasion offers you a new opportunity for vindictiveness. For instance, why not try a Christmas card that says:

"May your Christmas jewelry be the first thing that turns green in the spring."

In *Romeo and Juliet,* Shakespeare came up with a lovely wedding curse, "A plague on both your houses."
A more modern version might be:

"May your honeymoon plane be hijacked so that you spend your wedding night in the Djakarta airport."

You can curse an anniversary:

"May your wife understand you."

A good curse for somebody who is about to retire after 45 years of faithful service to the same company:

"May your retirement plan be supervised by Jimmy Hoffa."

Remember: No occasion is too small for your large hatreds.

NOW YOU'RE ON YOUR OWN

And now at last—O Sultan of Sadism, Vizier of Viciousness, Prince of Punishment, King of Kurses—having completed our course of instruction, you are ready to launch your own career in contumely.

As you go out of these unhallowed halls of hatred today, dear graduate, consider this last example of the techniques we have so laboriously taught you.

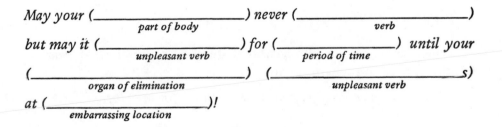

May your (_____) never (_____)
                    part of body   *verb*
but may it (_____) for (_____) until your
                unpleasant verb   *period of time*
(_____) (_____s)
        organ of elimination   *unpleasant verb*
at (_____)!
        embarrassing location

And if you haven't learned anything from this book then, "Curses! May you be foiled again and again and again!"

"A bad end should catch up with you."